Original title:
Sprouting Secrets

Copyright © 2025 Creative Arts Management OÜ
All rights reserved.

Author: Henry Beaumont
ISBN HARDBACK: 978-1-80566-763-6
ISBN PAPERBACK: 978-1-80566-833-6

Rooted in Disguise

In the garden, whispers play,
A radish wears a mask today.
Carrots chuckle, squinting green,
What's the funniest thing they've seen?

Turnips twirl in silly hats,
Telling tales of sneaky cats.
Cabbages hold a karaoke night,
While peas pretend they're taking flight.

The Offbeat Dance of Germination

In the soil, a party brews,
Who knew roots could share the news?
Dance like nobody's in sight,
Wiggle-wobble, what a fright!

With a beet in polka dots,
And a sunflower doing knots.
The daffodils break out in cheer,
As sprouts throw confetti, oh dear!

From Darkness to Light

In the gloom, the seeds all yawn,
"Let's grow wild, by the dawn!"
Potatoes giggle, snug in their beds,
While onions plot with funny heads.

The Unfolding Narrative

In garden beds, secrets unfold,
A tale of beans and marigolds.
Tomatoes gossip in the sun,
"Who's the funniest? Let's have fun!"

With stories sprouting, here and there,
Each leaf a laugh, each root a dare.
So come, dear friends, join in the jest,
In the thriving earth, we're truly blessed!

The Silent Bloom

In a garden where whispers play,
Pansies giggle in bright array.
A daisy dons a silly frown,
While the roses just clown around.

The tulips sway in teasing mock,
Tickling bees with their soft talk.
Sneaky sprouts peek from below,
Ready to join the laugh-out show.

Leaves giggle, sharing a jest,
As the sun aims to do its best.
In this plot of joy and cheer,
Nature's fun is ever near.

Watch the vines now twist and twirl,
With mushrooms dancing in a whirl.
In this quirky leafy spree,
Every plant has glee to see.

Threads of Nature

A spider spins with crafty grace,
In nature's thread, a funny chase.
He winks at flies, oh what a mess,
His webs are tales of sheer excess.

Petals whisper tales of glee,
As ants march by, they giggle free.
They trip on roots, it's quite a sight,
Nature's chaos brings pure delight.

In a fern's fold, a squirrel peeks,
He steals the scene with nutty tricks.
Laughter echoes through the glade,
As even shadows start to fade.

With every breeze, the grass has fun,
Join the dance beneath the sun.
Threads of joy through nature weave,
In this world, all hearts believe.

Secrets of the Ground

Underneath where giants creep,
The worms are holding secrets deep.
They giggle in their squirmy huddle,
As we stomp around in our muddle.

Mice share whispers with each mole,
Plotting mischief in their hole.
But oh, that clever little bug,
Turns a thistle into a snug hug.

Roots plot pranks, on top they tease,
Poking fun at passing bees.
A mushroom giggles, feeling grand,
Telling tales of a fairy land.

So, watch your step in this dark place,
Where laughter hides with a sly face.
In the soil, surprises abound,
Oh, the fun that's underground!

The Hidden Awakening

In chilly dawn, the sprouts awake,
Tickled by dew, they bend and shake.
Beneath the surface, a silly jig,
Nature's secrets, wise and big.

A dandelion's hairdo is wild,
Prancing around like a carefree child.
While ladybugs boast of their speed,
In a race that plants never heed.

Trees chuckle as squirrels collide,
With acorns bouncing, oh what a ride!
The sun peeks in, a friendly prank,
As shadows dance, a cheerful prank.

Every bud holds a playful cheer,
Old roots giggle, drawing near.
In this riot of green and hue,
The hidden laughs are meant for you.

Beneath the Surface

A potato dreamed of being grand,
But found itself in muddy land.
With visions of a shiny skin,
It schemed with peas to sneak a grin.

Carrots danced beneath the dirt,
While radishes wore shirts to flirt.
They tickled worms with leafy jokes,
And giggled loud, those crafty folks.

At night, the beetroot sang a tune,
Beneath the stars, beneath the moon.
In secret halls where veggies meet,
They hatch their plans with roots so sweet.

Nature's Quiet Confessions

The bushes whisper tales bizarre,
Of squirrels who think they own the bar.
With acorn hats and tiny beers,
They toast to all their gathered fears.

A flower overheard the chat,
About a cat who wore a hat.
It giggled petals, swayed a bit,
And wondered where that feline fit.

The trees, they chuckled as they swayed,
At all the silly pranks they played.
They peeked at roots both shy and bold,
Confessing secrets long untold.

The Unseen Bloom

In shadows thick, the daisies plot,
To bloom at dawn, but not a spot.
They wear disguises, just for fun,
And laugh as breezes steal their sun.

The violets scheme with shrubs nearby,
To catch the clouds that float on by.
With paintbrush skills, they try and try,
To color in the sunny sky.

Hidden blooms with winks and sighs,
Conspire softly 'neath the skies.
As bees are fooled by fragrant lies,
They dance in joy, and none despise.

Footprints in the Fertile Earth

The garden gnomes played hide and seek,
While worms concocted plans unique.
A rabbit raced with carrots bright,
Leaving footprints in the night.

The ladybugs wore polka dots,
And laughed at all the tangled knots.
In every thump of little feet,
Was evidence of their lost treat.

As crickets chirped a silly song,
The flowers joined to cheer along.
With every wiggle, twist, and shout,
They marked the earth with joy, no doubt.

Echoes of Possibility

In the garden where whispers play,
Seeds giggle and dance all day.
Bugs wear hats, bees sing tunes,
Even the sun joins in at noon.

Worms in tuxedos twist and slide,
While daisies gossip with great pride.
Every leaf has tales to tell,
In this haven where laughter dwells.

The Garden's Unfolding

Tomatoes wink in the morning light,
Zucchini crack jokes with all their might.
Radishes dress in hues so bright,
They might just steal the show tonight!

The peas make puns, climbing up high,
While carrots lay flat, oh me, oh my!
A garden party, no guest list required,
Just come with laughter, and your hearts inspired.

Silent Revelations of Nature

Under leaves where secrets nap,
Squirrels play chess, and take a nap.
Mushrooms sprout in polka dot styles,
While flowers trade secrets and smiles.

The breeze tells tales of yore and lore,
As shadows dance on the forest floor.
A playful nudge from nature's breeze,
Reminds us all to laugh with ease.

The Nature of Secrets

In the thicket, a secret's a chuckle,
Where snails race for fun, what a struggle!
Petunias plot under starry skies,
While crickets leap with surprise.

The moon rolls her eyes at the cheeky flies,
As frogs croak jokes, oh such good tries!
In this realm of the green and the wild,
Nature's a playground, spirited and wild.

The Hidden Symphony of Growth

In the garden, plants do dance,
Whispering tales of chance,
Worms wear hats, oh what a sight,
Beetles play jazz every night.

A sunflower spins like a top,
While carrots sway and hops won't stop,
Raindrops chuckle, seeds take flight,
In this symphony, pure delight.

Leaves of Memory

Fallen leaves have tales to tell,
Of squirrels' mischief, quite a hell,
They float and twirl on breezy days,
In leafy laughter, nature plays.

One cheeky nut forgot his stash,
While fungi giggle in a flash,
Memories rustle, breezes tease,
Of chipmunks prancing with such ease.

Tapestry of the Undergrowth

In shadows deep, the gnomes convene,
Knitting tales of mossy green,
A tapestry of giggles spun,
Where mushrooms laugh and sunlight's fun.

Crickets chirp their secret codes,
While sleepy flowers play the toads,
In this weave of life so bright,
Even weeds know how to delight.

Cultivated Treasures

Tucked in soil like a treasure chest,
Potatoes plot and peas protest,
With every sprout, a merry cheer,
Radishes joke, 'We're growing here!'

Tomatoes blush in summer sun,
While garlic whispers, 'This is fun!'
In garden beds, where laughter grows,
Every veggie has its shows.

Germinating Dreams

In the garden of my mind, so spry,
A cabbage wears a silly tie.
With carrots playing hide and seek,
They giggle softly, too shy to speak.

Tomatoes dance a wobbly jig,
While radishes proclaim, "I'm big!"
They toss confetti, leaves afloat,
In the soil where dreamers gloat.

A gnome with glasses reads a book,
He finds it quite a funny nook.
With mushrooms laughing, quite absurd,
The wise old sage just shakes and spurred.

So plant your thoughts in soil of cheer,
And watch your dreams grow year by year!

Unraveling the Green

In a patch of peas, a joke was spun,
A bean replied, "I'm just a pun!"
With squirrels chuckling in delight,
The lettuce winks, it's quite a sight.

A flower whispers, "What's the deal?"
As carrots giggle, "Do we feel real?"
The radish shimmies, oh what glee,
As bees all buzz, "Just let us be!"

With roots that tickle underground,
The spinach laughs at what they've found.
A cabbage rolls, and oh my, look!
He's got the rhubarb's recipe book!

So in this garden, life's a blast,
Where every sprout has fun amassed!

Mystical Sprouts

In twilight's glow, a seedling grins,
It tells a tale of leafy sins.
A flower boasts of magic tricks,
While dancing gnomes pull silly pricks.

The sunflowers, tall, play peek-a-boo,
With whispers strange, they know what's true.
"Let's form a band," the onions cheer,
While radishes hum, "We'll make it clear!"

With soil as thick as cake, oh my!
The peas all gather, ready to fly.
They bounce and hop from bud to bud,
And chuckle softly into the mud.

So let your sprouts strut, let them show,
For in this garden, laughter will grow!

Whispers in the Wind

A breeze tickles the leafy crew,
The chives complain, "What is our due?"
The daisies giggle, "Don't you pout!"
While worms laugh loud, "Just hear us out!"

A sunflower shouts, "I'm the king!"
To pumpkins rolling, it's a fling!
With every nudged seed, joy unfolds,
In stories that the earth beholds.

Potatoes grumble, buried so deep,
While up above, the shadows creep.
Yet every sprout sings with delight,
As petals twirl to greet the night.

So listen close, beneath the moon,
Where laughter grows and dreams are strewn!

Seeds of Curiosity

In the garden of thoughts, a seed took a trip,
Wiggling and giggling, on a little leaf slip.
It whispered to daisies, a riddle or two,
"Why do the bees buzz? What else could they do?"

The carrots grew shy, taking digs at the peas,
"Why do you all laugh? We're not meant to tease!"
The radishes snickered, forming a club,
"Join us for mischief, no need for a shrub!"

Enigmatic Tendrils

Wiggly vines danced, like they'd drunk too much juice,
Looping and swooping, they had no excuse.
They tangled up tulips in a tricky embrace,
"Watch out for the butterflies, they're all over the place!"

With potions of sunlight, they mixed and they twirled,
Creating a ruckus, a vine-spiral world.
"I'll be your partner," cried one bright green stem,
"Let's weave a tall tale; come join in my gem!"

Nature's Confession

A squirrel once blurted, "I've got a big stash,
Of acorns and secrets, and oh, such a splash!"
The trees leaned in closer, with branches all perked,
"Tell us your tales, or we'll go nuts, you jerk!"

"Alright, alright!" said the squirrel quite shy,
"I've kept some good gossip about the sky!
Did you know the clouds are just fluff on a spree?
They giggle and tumble, like you and me!"

Unseen Horizons

Beyond the tall grasses, where the wild things play,
Whispers of adventures float on breezes that sway.
There's a party of critters, all dressed in bold hues,
With snacks made of sunshine and sparkling dew!

The hedgehogs are dancing, they rolled out their spines,
While crickets draw straws for the best punchline.
"Who's bringing the cupcakes? The party's no fun!"
"If we can't see them, then why should we run?"

Shadows of Growth

In the garden where veggies conspire,
A tomato tells tales of its tire.
The carrots giggle with leafy delight,
While beans plot a dance in the moonlight.

Radishes whisper, their tops all aflame,
About how they once played a silly game.
Potatoes chuckle, stuck in the ground,
As onions reveal how they're rotten, profound.

With each double twist and a snickered glance,
The zucchinis join in for a wild dance.
Eggplants ponder their purple despair,
While lettuce just laughs with a ruffled hair.

In this hidden plot, fun grows every day,
Where secrets abound and mischief holds sway.
So come take a peek, and you might just see,
The laughter of plants, so wild and so free.

The Language of Roots

Down in the soil, where the secrets reside,
Roots chat in whispers, they can't help but chide.
A gnarled old oak shares a cheeky tale,
While spritely young shoots start waving without fail.

"Did you see how the weeds tried to snoop?
They stumbled and fell, what a clumsy troop!"
The daisies giggle, "We're no simple bunch,
We're blooming thinkers, we're just on a hunch!"

A dandelion's wish floats on the breeze,
It hopes for some rain but would settle for cheese!
The roots chuckle softly, they all have a plan,
To let out more secrets than any plant can.

So next time you wander where gardens convene,
Listen closely to whispers, just like a dream.
For under the surface, delight often lurks,
In the playful exchanges of nature's quirks.

Veiled Revelations

In a patch where the orchids throw shade,
Lies a secret that no one has laid.
The violets gossip with petals that flare,
"Oh my, did you hear? That cactus is bare!"

Behind all the ferns, a wild rumor spreads,
That tulips wear hats whenever they're wed.
The peonies blush, their petals turn pink,
As daisies confess, "We can all really stink!"

"All this hot gossip, let's plant it anew,
For sprouts in the spring will remember it too!"
The posies all scheme with a whimsical strut,
To mix up the truth, oh, what a big cut!

So if you are strolling through blooms that confound,
Pay heed to the secrets that scatter around.
For in every petal, a joke might just land,
And laughter can blossom where laughter is planned.

Dormant Wishes

In the quiet of beds where the lilies lie low,
Dreams of the seasons begin to bestow.
The tulips are daydreaming of colors so bright,
While crocuses chuckle at the last winter fight.

"Shall we dance in the rain? Oh, what a grand night!"
Said the daffodils rising, with petals in sight.
But the shy little bulbs, still tucked out of view,
Are planning a party, all covered in dew.

With rhymes in the air and giggles galore,
Each bud hides a wish behind every door.
"Let's tease the old daisies with grasshopper hops,
And spin tales of fairies with enormous lollipops!"

So next time you wander through gardens untamed,
Know laughter is waiting where secrets are claimed.
For dreams in the soil grow stories so fine,
In the whimsical whispers, let hilarity shine.

Intricate Life Beneath

In the soil, whispers play,
Worms gossip night and day.
Roots make puns, tickle the ground,
Laughing softly without a sound.

Grubs who dance like they're on fire,
Claiming they all have a choir.
Fungi strut with hats of flair,
Mushrooms giggle in the air.

Critters plot their grand parade,
Ants in suits, aren't they a trade?
Beetles boast of their great weight,
"Look at me!" they jokingly state.

All around, secrets sown,
In this realm, they've found a home.
Life below, a laugh-filled fest,
Where every creature shows its best.

Nature's Layered Narrative

In the leaves, a tale unfolds,
Chipmunks giggle, secrets told.
Squirrels on a treasure quest,
Nuts and acorns are their chest.

Raccoons wear their masks with pride,
Waddling with their loot beside.
Nature's pranks, a playful twist,
Creatures dance, they can't resist.

Mice in coats of patchy brown,
Have a tea party, all renown.
"Do you prefer sugar or spice?"
"Both!" they squeak, "A fine advice!"

Underneath the grassy waves,
Whiskers twitch, clever knaves.
Nature whispers, shares a grin,
Beneath our feet, the fun begins.

Undercurrents of Life

Down in the muck, life lets loose,
Tadpoles exchange their juicy moose.
"Ribbit, ribbit!" they take a leap,
Sharing laughs, no time for sleep.

Fish flip-flop, making a splash,
Vying for the biggest cache.
Algae's buzzing, "What's your game?"
"Just swimming!" they all exclaim.

Underwater rock-star pets,
Guppies claim their big regrets.
"Did I forget to wash my fins?"
They chuckle hard, as misstep grins.

In the depths where few may tread,
Life's a party, full of thread.
Hidden joys, the bubbles rise,
In the currents, laughter flies.

Fertile Confidences

In the garden, gossip blooms,
Petals sharing all their dooms.
"Did you see that bee up close?"
"Buzzing by like they're the most!"

Carrots blushing, underground spies,
Whisper tales of sunny skies.
Tomatoes smirk, all dressed in red,
"Ripe and juicy, that's what we said!"

Pumpkins plotting Halloween,
"Let's scare kids, oh what a scene!"
Radishes giggle, round and spry,
"Hide me deep, I don't want to die!"

Beans ascend with humor's touch,
"Climb it high, it won't cost much!"
Fertile tales in every nook,
In this patch, all are off the hook.

Veils of Verdant Growth

In a garden where whispers dance,
A broccoli's wearing a cabbage's pants.
With lettuce giggles and radish pranks,
The cucumbers giggle in leafy ranks.

The beans tell tales with a jolly twist,
While carrots plot, and none can resist.
Tomatoes wear hats made of bright sun,
As peas have a party and not just for fun.

A flower complains of being too sweet,
While herbs exchange secrets with a cheeky greet.
Chives hide the truth with their fragrant breath,
And cilantro can't keep quiet, avoiding death.

When the garden's at play, it's a sly charade,
Each plant a comedian in leafy brigade.
With roots in the ground, they're up to some tricks,
In this verdant world where humor picks.

Shadows in the Sunlight

Underneath the big oak's shade,
A squirrel tells stories that throw us dismayed.
The shadows are laughing, causing a fuss,
As sunbeams bounce in a hushed discussions.

With dandelions singing in hoarse, high notes,
They gossip of gardens and trouble afloat.
The fairies giggle, covering their peeking,
While worms play charades, and mushrooms are squeaking.

Who knew the sun could tickle the ground?
With secrets so silly, they twirl all around.
Caterpillars joke of their butterfly fate,
As beetles roll laughter on soft, sandy plates.

In this world where the shadows delight,
Squirrels are jesters, the sun is polite.
Every nook holds a chuckle, a wink, and a nudge,
In a dance where the wild keeps laughing as judge.

The Language of Leaves

Leaves are chattering in the breezy air,
Trading stories, without a care.
With each rustle, a joke takes flight,
They whisper secrets in the cool moonlight.

A maple's making fun of the stubborn oak,
While birches giggle at a shy little yoke.
The ferns are snickering, waving their fronds,
As ivy sneaks in with cheeky respond.

Each leaf is a voice in the great leafy scheme,
Crafting a chorus, like a leafy dream.
With playful banter so light and amusing,
Their laughter catches the sunlight, infusing.

So next time you stroll through the lush green maze,
Listen closely to the leaves' funny plays.
For under their shade, the humor does bloom,
In the fanciful whispers where joy finds room.

Revelations in the Petals

In a garden where petals delight,
Roses are rolling, ready to fight.
Daisies debate which one's the best,
While tulips are busy in a friendly jest.

Lily pads laugh at the toads by the brook,
Trading wisecracks under every nook.
Petals are gossiping with such little care,
Each one has a story, a secret to share.

Sunflowers boast of their height with pride,
While poppies paint dreams on the grassy glide.
With fluttering fun and a bright splash of color,
The blooms weave tales, each one like a baller.

When petals unite for a carnival show,
They laugh at the breeze, putting on a glow.
In this bouquet of secrets, hilarity thrives,
With every bright bloom, the joy comes alive.

Secrets of the Leaf

In the garden with a giggle,
Leaves play hide and seek, with a wiggle.
One claims it's a dragon in disguise,
The other just chuckles, 'What a surprise!'

Rain droplets hold whispers, so dear,
Telling tales only flowers can hear.
A beetle decides to join the chat,
"How did I become such a fancy brat?"

In shadows, the roots begin to plot,
Napping plants dream of the treasure they've got.
Beneath the soil, a dance starts to bloom,
As worms shake their tails in a silty ballroom.

At sunset, the petals giggle and sway,
Sharing secrets of joy at the end of the day.
Nature's comedians, both sly and spry,
Chuckle together as the night drifts by.

Hidden Currents

In streams where the fish put on a show,
They boast of the places that they go.
One guy brags, "I've danced with a leaf!"
All the others roll eyes in disbelief.

The turtles hold court and decide in style,
'We'll paddle in circles; just wait a while!'
With wink and a nudge, they craft a plan,
To outsmart the heron, the feathery man.

Moss cushions the rocks like a cozy bed,
Squirrels exchange gossip, it's well-read.
"Did you hear what the brook babbled last night?"
"Just rumors about frogs and their leap of delight."

When ripples start giggling in the sun,
All the pond dwellers know that it's time for fun.
With bubbles and splashes, a comical spree,
Nature's soap opera, as grand as can be.

The Intrigue of Growth

Once a sprout in a pot so small,
Dreamed of adventures, brave and gall.
'Will I be a tree? A leafy delight?'
All the weeds laughed, 'You'll never take flight!'

But little did they know, I had my scheme,
Water and sunlight fueled my dream.
I stretched and I tugged with a giggle of glee,
'Watch out! Here I come, all green and free!'

With each inch I gained, the competition gasped,
As I twisted and turned, fun firmly clasped.
'Who knew growth could be such a lark?'
I winked at the daisies, "Let's dance in the park."

As blossoms burst forth, colors so bright,
The garden erupted in joy and delight.
Nature's comedy written in shades so bold,
A tale of sprouting, aptly retold.

Lurking Potential

Beneath the surface, where mischief brews,
A potato plotted to break the news.
'One day I'll sprout and dance in the sun,
While you judge me harshly, I'll have my fun!'

In darkness, the beans traded a wink,
"We'll twist up the fence and give folks a stink."
Their giggles echoed, planning their flight,
A green tower blooming by morning light.

Old carrots, wise, chuckled away,
"Just wait for spring; it's our kind of play!"
Buried deep, they formed a council of jest,
"Let's put on a show; we'll outshine the rest!"

As winter fades, whispers arise,
Each tiny sprout stretches, reaching for skies.
With laughter unrooted, they break through the ground,
In a garden of gags, where fun can abound.

Whispers Beneath the Soil

In the garden, whispers flow,
Worms gossip, oh what a show!
Roots tickle, plants hold tight,
Beneath the ground, it's quite a sight.

Chickens cluck with haughty flair,
Raccoons dance without a care.
Bees buzz tales of fragrant blooms,
While carrots plot their leafy tunes.

A squirrel buries secrets deep,
In a corner, he won't keep.
As daisies giggle at the sun,
They make the flowers laugh and run.

Beneath the leaves, a grand parade,
Of silly bugs in masquerade.
In this world of roots and sprouts,
Laughter grows, no room for doubts.

Hidden Truths in the Garden

Amidst the trowels and the spade,
A gnome tells jokes, he's quite the aid.
Pumpkin heads with grinning glee,
Share tales of what the bees all see.

Tomatoes blush from all the fun,
As rabbits race just like the sun.
Rogue turnips plotting midnight snacks,
While marigolds guard hidden tracks.

A sneaky fox peeks from the grass,
Hoping all the gossip won't pass.
The roses laugh, they know it's true,
Every bloom has a tale or two.

Under leaves where shadows play,
Secrets giggle through the day.
Laughter sprouts like daisies wild,
In the garden, we're all beguiled.

Echoes of the Seed

Seeds whisper softly in the breeze,
Telling stories of their trees.
Cabbages dream on the chilly ground,
While onions tease with layers found.

The daffodils, all dressed in cheer,
Bounce and bob for all to hear.
Side by side, they dance and sway,
Spreading jokes with every ray.

A lazy dog sprawls in the shade,
Dreaming up a garden parade.
Frogs croak puns on lily pads,
While crickets laugh at silly fads.

The sun peeks out, a warm surprise,
As leaves exchange their witty lies.
In this world where laughter grows,
A merry tune in nature flows.

Unraveled Mysteries of Spring

Springtime giggles in the air,
As the flowers dress with flair.
Buds unfold with chatter bright,
Sharing giggles day and night.

A cheeky bee dons a tiny hat,
Buzzing secrets to the cat.
Lettuce lounges in the sun,
A lazy plant, just having fun.

Chickens crack the funniest jokes,
While the daisies play with pokes.
In this land of rooty cheer,
Even weeds join in, oh dear!

Vines twist stories, oh so grand,
Nature's humor, hand in hand.
In every petal, laughter dwells,
As springtime weaves its playful spells.

Tapestry of Green

In gardens where whispers do bloom,
A cabbage dances, dispelling all gloom.
With lettuce grins and radish winks,
They plot their mischief over drinks.

The carrots convene, lost in cheer,
Swapping tall tales as worms draw near.
A rogue with a hat, the brussels sprout shouts,
"We're not just veggies, we've got clout!"

As sunlight spills honey, a beet starts to sing,
While peas play guitar, oh the joy that they bring.
Cucumbers giggle, all dressed in their green,
In this party of leaves, no one's ever mean!

With every quick rustle, a secret's revealed,
The truth behind greens, forever concealed.
A kaleidoscope world, wild and spry,
Where veggies unite and laughter runs high.

Nourishing the Unknown

In the depths of dark soil, tales grow old,
Of broccoli dreams and secrets untold.
Beets blush from gossip like roots in the clay,
Follow those whispers, they lead you astray.

Radishes chirp with their crimson delight,
Plotting their pranks both day and night.
"We'll dress up the sprouts in grand feathered hats,"
Cried out the chives, while dodging the cats.

Here's to the beans that sway to the beat,
As they practice their dance with two left feet.
They'll shimmy and jump, then trip on a vine,
Laughing at spills, it's a grand old time!

The cucumbers snicker, just hide and reveal,
Each squishy delight a comical meal.
In this feast of the fun, all flavors collide,
With greenery giggles, joy can't be denied.

Petals of Insight

In gardens of giggles, the petals tell tales,
Of daisies that dream in frilly frail veils.
A sunflower yawns, stretching tall to the sun,
"This patch is to laugh—why walk when we run?"

Buttercups play as they tickle the breeze,
While lilacs conspire, bringing bushes to tease.
A daffodil dares, with a brave little dance,
"Join me, my friends, let's give spring a chance!"

Lily pads leap, on ponds all aglow,
With tadpoles that giggle in waters below.
They splash and they dart, each secret they share,
Nature's own mischief is found everywhere.

So while arms are outstretched and shadows do play,
Remember the blooms that brighten your day.
In laughter we thrive, in petals we find,
The joy of the garden, where secrets unwind.

The Secret Life of Flora

In the hidden realm of leafy delight,
Herbs chat and chuckle from morning to night.
Pepper plants gossip about tomato's flair,
While sage rolls its eyes, so sassy and rare.

Chives hold a meeting beneath a big moon,
Discussing the antics of poor little prune.
"Why do veggies hide what's green under the dirt?"
"Because they fear salad—oh, it can hurt!"

Insects are spies, eavesdropping there,
On flowers' wild plans for a whimsical fair.
With petals as banners and roots as their crew,
A funky parade no one knows, just a few!

So, should you wander and come upon green,
Remember the laughter that buzzes between.
Nature's own mischief, in leaves it will linger,
Tap into the fun, just follow the finger!

Tales from the Root's Embrace

In the garden's heart lies a rubber chicken,
Rooted deep, it starts its quakin'.
The daisies giggle as the tulips sway,
'Why choose a fowl for a garden play?'

A rumor spreads among the weeds,
That carrots dance when no one sees.
The radishes blush beneath the soil,
While broccoli dreams of a veggie royal.

Cabbages bask in a leafy mess,
Whispering tales of garden stress.
A gopher grins, with a sneaky plot,
"Don't tell the squash, but I like it hot!"

In this patch of green, laughter takes root,
As every sprout sings its silly loot.
From the depths of earth to the skies so blue,
A chorus of veggies, all wacky, yet true.

Secrets of the Budding Branch

Beneath the boughs of a curious tree,
A squirrel plays tricks, just wait and see.
Swinging on branches, he drops acorns,
While the flowers blush in pastel scorns.

'What's that sound?' asks the shy old moss,
'Just the bugs planning their new gloss.'
Sunflowers wink at the passing bees,
Sharing giggles with the whispering leaves.

A bird with style, sporting a hat,
Sings of adventures, and just where he sat.
The wind tells secrets to those who share,
As laughter floats lightly through sun-kissed air.

In the shade of this secretive land,
Every twist of fate is subtly planned.
The trees conspire, they twist, they dance,
Creating a world of whimsical chance.

Seeds of Silence

In a quiet patch where silence hums,
Tiny seeds gather, they wiggle and drum.
They whisper about the sun's warm glow,
And plot a performance for all to show.

A lone potato thinks he's a star,
While beans debate how high they'll go far.
'Let's leave the dirt,' says a plucky pea,
'For today's play, we shall dance with glee!'

The herbs in the corner roll their eyes,
"Are you all nuts? How boring it lies."
But the thyme knows best, with a twinkle bright,
"Time for some action under the moonlight!"

So the seeds take a leap, they hop all around,
With laughter exploding from underground.
Shy little sprouts join the jubilant show,
In a silent space, where joy starts to grow.

The Garden's Enigma

In the garden's depths, a mystery blooms,
Where gnomes huddle tight in leafy rooms.
They plot and they scheme with cheeky delight,
Crafting solutions to win the night.

The broccoli whispers to the peas on diet,
"Just wait till the cabbage, now that's a riot!"
The carrots giggle, all orange and bright,
"Who knew we'd be funny? It feels so right!"

A parsnip claims he's a rare ancient sage,
While rhubarb quips, "You're just on a stage!"
In this playful realm of veggies galore,
Comics of root and leaf, never a bore!

So raise your trowels, let's dig up the fun,
In a garden where laughter is never outdone.
With every bloom comes a tale to unspool,
In the enigma of green, beneath nature's rule.

Soft Murmurs

In the garden, whispers rise,
Plants giggle, nature's surprise.
Worms below, tune their show,
Tickling roots as they go.

Petals dance in afternoon,
Bees beatbox, buzzing a tune.
Gnomes gossip 'neath the rose,
Sharing tales that no one knows.

Sunbeams peek through leafy hats,
Squirrels jive amidst the chats.
Hummingbirds flaunt their flair,
In this party, all are there.

Laughter grows in every nook,
Every vine's a playful hook.
Here in soil, the fun's not thin,
Mysteries where grins begin.

Fragrant Hints

A whiff of mischief in the air,
Daisies winking without a care.
Jasmine spills its secret scent,
As dandelions cheer, all content.

Roses wear their blush of pink,
While daisies tease with winks and blinks.
Lavender nods, a sly little sprite,
In this perfume, day turns into night.

Sunshine tickles the petals' cheeks,
Pansies giggle, nature speaks.
With every breeze, a hint of fun,
A garden's laughter has just begun.

Fragrant whispers, sly and free,
In the blooms, a jubilee.
Nature's chuckles all around,
Where every scent is laughter found.

The Secret Garden of Hope

Behind the hedges, laughter spills,
Mice with dreams and daffodil thrills.
Every leaf's a chuckle, it seems,
In this nook where sunlight beams.

Sunflowers wear their crowns so bright,
Swaying, they dance with pure delight.
Bumblebees in tiny suits,
Jazzing up the roots with hoots.

Ladybugs roll, tiny and round,
In this wonder, joy abounds.
Frogs in tuxedos croak their tune,
All united under the moon.

Hope's a flower that's bursting wide,
In laughter's lap, we all abide.
With roots of joy and blooms of cheer,
This secret spot is always near.

Underground Symphony

Below the ground, the laughter grows,
Wiggly worms strike up their prose.
Roots tap dance in underground halls,
While moles beat drums with tiny calls.

Rats compose with cheese-filled chords,
Their melody, nature's rewards.
Ants march in a rhythmic line,
A bustling, jolly, secret sign!

Every burrow holds a tune,
Shaking soil to the light of the moon.
The underground is quite a sight,
With critters playing through the night.

Join the band with leaf and twig,
As laughter flows, and spirits dig.
In this symphony, life takes wing,
Where nature's music makes us sing.

The Covered Awakening

Underneath the leafy veil,
A squirrel danced and told a tale,
Of hiding nuts, a secret stash,
He thought it clever, oh so bash!

A peep from roots, a giggle low,
A worm popped out, putting on a show,
'I've seen your stash!' it teased with glee,
'We'll share a nut, just you and me!'

Then ants arrived, a marching band,
'Your secret's ours, ain't that just grand?'
With tiny drums they played so loud,
While the squirrel burst, but oh, so proud!

And when the sun began to set,
The squirrel winked, 'No need to fret,'
A new growth sprouted, bold and spry,
The great reveal beneath the sky!

Inflorescence of Insight

Bees buzzing tales of sweet delight,
Fluttering blooms, oh what a sight!
A daisy yelled, 'I'm in the know!'
But laugh it off, it's just for show.

A gardener stumbled on the scene,
Mistaking weeds for something green,
The flowers snickered all around,
As the garden clown fell to the ground.

'You think you know,' said sly old rose,
'But I have secrets nobody knows!'
She whispered low, with petals spread,
While leafy friends just shook their heads.

In this patch of floral cheer,
The truths unwind, but not one tear,
A world of whimsy, fun so bright,
Where every bud can join the light!

Nature's Quiet Story

In the forest's hush, a tale unfolds,
Of quirky critters, bold and bold,
A raccoon's hat, a misfit's pride,
With laughter echoing far and wide.

Beneath the brush, a laugh ignite,
As bunnies hash their plans by night,
'What's hidden here?' one twitching nose,
A giggle escaped from ticklish toes.

Owls hoot softly, wise with jest,
Sharing jokes while taking rest,
'The moon's our friend, let's not delay!'
With whispers of fun till break of day.

So listen close, the trees engage,
Each rustle turns another page,
Nature's symphony plays everywhere,
With secrets hidden, light as air!

Enchanted Endings

A sunset winked, a cheeky sight,
While stars began their twinkling flight,
A turtle smiled, 'It's time to part,'
With dreams and giggles, a merry heart.

The crickets chirp their evening tune,
A firefly danced beneath the moon,
As nature's jesters speak their lines,
In shadows where the laughter shines.

Each whisper winds through nighttime air,
Unraveling secrets lying bare,
Where every creature plays a role,
In this enchanted, merry stroll.

So let the night weave stories bright,
Of endless giggles out of sight,
For as the stars come out to play,
The magic grows, come what may!

The Soul of the Seed

In the dark, a tiny sprout,
Whispers of what life's about.
It giggles at the dirt so deep,
Curled up tight, it starts to peep.

With a wink to the warm sun,
It dreams of green, oh what fun!
Yet, its friends just shake their heads,
"You'll need more than just your beds!"

The raindrops play a merry tune,
Dancing lightly, like a loon.
"Come join our frolicking mass!"
The seed just smiles, ``I'll pass!``

In this race to reach the sky,
Who knew dirt was so awry?
But here it grows, inside the clover,
With every chuckle, it gets bolder!

Leafy Confidences

High upon a branch so bold,
Leaves discuss the tales untold.
"I caught a glimpse of a squirrel's stash!"
"And I saw Rory's big crash!"

With breezy laughs, they spin and twirl,
Each one vying for the swirl.
"Did you hear what the raindrops said?"
"They dream of flowers, not of dread!"

Gossip flows in rustling tones,
As they dance, steering clear of drones.
"The wind is such an airy joker!"
"It tickled me, I'm such a choker!"

They plot and scheme as shadows fall,
A leafy council, laughter's call.
"Let's prank that sleepy old tree!"
"Leafy antics, can't wait to see!"

The Unspoken Harvest

In the garden, things are rife,
Banter blooms, it's a leafy life.
"Hey turnip, what's your story today?"
"Not much, just growing—what can I say?"

With tomatoes rolling, feeling grand,
"We're the stars of this summer band!"
But radishes pipe up, jesting clear,
"Dare to challenge? We won't shed a tear!"

Then sudden chaos, true delight!
The veggies plot through day and night.
"We'll showcase our colors in a flash!"
"But who'll steal this sweet, sweet stash?"

With laughter echoing, crops unite,
Harvest moon, a joyful sight.
They thrive in games both wise and witty,
In the end, it's just pure city!

Roots of Revelation

Deep below, where whispers roam,
Roots hold secrets, making home.
"Did you hear? The tops are wild!"
"They're having fun like every child!"

With grumbles low and giggles tight,
Roots stretch wide in the dim twilight.
"Oh, to be up, swaying free!"
"While we soldier on, hidden glee!"

A gopher tumbles, gives a cheer,
"Revealed it all, now the drought's near!"
Roots quiver, shake off their gloom,
"Let's tease them back, inside this tomb!"

Through tangled tales and whispered arts,
These roots find joy, they play their parts.
A soil saga of laughs abound,
In silence, the deepest joys are found!

Breaths of New Life

A seed in the ground, oh what a surprise,
With dreams of the sky and sun on its eyes.
It wiggles and jigs, gives a curious dance,
While neighbors all wonder, is it a chance?

A worm gives a wink and says, "Look at me!"
Digging up dirt, oh what glee!
The sprout pops its head, says, "Watch out for flies!"
And waves to the bees, who hop by with their ties.

It stretches its leaves, all shiny and bright,
Says, "Don't take a nap, I'm the star of the night!"
With laughter and cheers from the bumblebee crew,
They toast with sweet nectar, who knew they could brew?

So here's to the joy of what's growing each day,
Life's little surprises that come out to play.
Through giggles and wiggles, we all like to cheer,
For a world full of wonders is always quite near.

The Quiet Bloom

In a garden so still, something tickled the air,
A bud had a secret, did anyone care?
It chuckled and rolled in its leafy cocoon,
While the daisies all danced to a slow, silly tune.

The sun made a joke, said, "What's green and round?"
A radish replied, "Now that's quite profound!"
Meanwhile, the bloom just giggled and swayed,
Deciding what color to wear for the day.

It peeked out at dragons, staring with glee,
Who thought they could scare it, too wild and free!
But the bloom just winked, like a star in the night,
And whispered, "Oh please, I'm the king of delight!"

So laughter blossomed where the colors collide,
Each flower a friend, in the giggling tide.
Nature's own playground, with secrets to share,
Bringing smiles and chuckles with sunshine to spare.

Nature's Hidden Chamber

Deep in the backyard, where shadows can play,
Lies a treasure of whispers that giggle all day.
The mushrooms hold secrets, all fuzzy and round,
While the daisies gossip without making a sound.

A rogue little squirrel gets caught in the act,
Sniffing the flowers, it's a comedic pact.
"What's in the sky?" asks a curious sprout,
"The whole world is wacky, come check it out!"

As raindrops tumble, they turn into cheer,
Each puddle reflects what the critters hold dear.
The secrets abound, in the soil and the roots,
With grasshoppers sharing their wise little toots.

So don't miss the fun that the garden can offer,
With laughter and joy, just like leafy scoffer.
Hidden beneath all the petals and vines,
Are giggly adventures in nature's designs.

Echoes of the Soil

In the heart of the earth, a riddle to find,
What sings to the worms and woos all the kind?
With roots making music, they twist and they turn,
While daisies are dancing, it's their time to churn.

The carrots are clamoring, "Don't eat us, we sing!"
While radishes giggle, say, "We've got the bling!"
And in this mad garden, where whispers abound,
Each seed has a story that's waiting unbound.

With chuckles from crickets who tap out a beat,
The blossoms all sway, with small nimble feet.
The soil starts to hum, as it stirs with delight,
Echoes of laughter fill up the night.

So cherish the sounds that sprout from the earth,
With jokes and with stories, we measure their worth.
For nature's a jester, with jokes yet untold,
Making merry the garden, a sight to behold.

Encoded in the Earth

In the dirt, they start to hum,
Worms play poker, feeling glum.
Seeds in coats, a fancy ball,
Whispers dance beneath it all.

One sprout sneezed, a flurry flew,
'Excuse me,' said the radish crew.
A carrot chuckled, 'What a sight!'
'Let's dig in, it's quite a night!'

The mushrooms wink, their jokes are rad,
Telling tales of dirt, not bad!
Roots strum tunes, a funky beat,
Nature's party, feel the heat!

So in the earth, where laughter's bred,
Watch out for giggles overhead.
Among the greens, the fun reveals,
That life erupts with silly feels.

Nature's Whispered Declarations

The daisies gossip, oh so sweet,
About the ants and how they cheat.
'Did you see that?' one flower spun,
'The beetles race, but who's the winner? None!'

Frogs croak laughs, their voices bold,
'We're the kings, or so we're told!'
While rabbits plot a carrot theft,
Nature holds secrets, cleverly kept.

Wind carries whispers, a breeze of jokes,
'Why did the tree dress up in cloaks?'
'To leaf the ground and seize the day!'
Nature's humor, hip-hip-hooray!

So listen close, the woods will tell,
Of silly antics and of spells.
In green disguise, the fun unfolds,
With laughter sung and stories told.

Layers of Life Beneath

Beneath the soil, they start to play,
Bugs bring snacks, and seeds relay.
'Pass the joke,' the grasses say,
'Before the sun begins to sway!'

The roots are tangled, a merry knot,
Each telling tales of all they've got.
The tulips giggle, 'Watch your feet!'
'Don't crush the fun, it's quite the treat!'

Worms wiggle-waggle, a dance so wild,
They joke about the leaves, and one sweet child.
'Why did the plant need a ride?',
'To leaf its roots and take a slide!'

Laughter echoes, as petals cheer,
In layers deep, the fun is clear.
Nature's jesters, alive and bright,
In every nook, the laughs take flight.

Germinating Wonders

Tiny sprouts wiggle in their beds,
Telling tales with leafy heads.
'What's up, grass?' a daisy winks,
'Let's share secrets with the drinks!'

A beetle breaks out a comedy show,
'Why don't plants ever go to snow?'
'Because they hate to chill and freeze,'
Nature's laughter whips through the trees.

The peas are rolling on the floor,
'Let's play hide and seek once more!'
With roots that tickle, and leaves that tease,
Nature's wonders, meant to please.

As sprouts break free, the world will see,
Humor flows wild, like a buzzing bee.
In every bud, a joke awaits,
In every root, a giggle creates.

Cryptic Growth

In the garden with weeds so tall,
I ask the daisies, 'Do you all talk?'
They giggle softly, swirling around,
Sharing tales of the worms underground.

A dandelion claims it's a royal bloom,
While ants plot the end of my broom.
They laugh at my half-hearted rattle,
While I wonder who's winning this battle.

The trowel listens, full of disdain,
At the gossip that grows like a train.
Every sprout has a story to tell,
In this wacky green, enchanted spell.

I sprinkle some seeds, a bit of fate,
Beware the plants that just can't wait.
They poke their heads with mischief and flair,
A leafy party, oh what a scare!

Secrets Beneath the Surface

In the soil where truths are veiled,
A cheeky root is slightly jailed.
It whispers, 'Hey, let's keep it sly,
I've seen the tomatoes give zucchini the eye!'

The carrots dance with the stubborn spud,
In a muddy floor, they're stuck in the crud.
'Can I get a hug?' pines the parsnip so bold,
While the radish just sighs, 'Oh, I'm too cold.'

The underground crew likes to play charades,
While the onions roll eyes in their leafy cascades.
Mushrooms giggle, as they leap from the dark,
Saying, 'What's life without a little spark?'

In this covert, cracked earthen dome,
Every seed knows a secret it calls home.
Through cracks and whispers they endlessly weave,
A garden with tales one cannot believe!

Hidden Flickers

Beneath the leaves a spark's a-stir,
Lightbugs gossip with a shining purr.
They flash in rhythm, teasing a tune,
As plants sway along, dancing to the moon.

A cheeky sprout talks big and bold,
Claims he's the rarest thing to behold.
He's just a weed with a major dream,
While the daisies giggle at the absurd scheme.

'Hey, watch me glow!' a firefly brags,
But the chives are rolling in holy rags.
As whispers flare within the shrub,
Wild laughter blooms where the critters hub.

A secret bloom waits to come alive,
In a world where the shyest thrive.
Underneath, the laughter flickers bright,
In this merry dance of the secret night.

Life's Delicate Unraveling

A daisy's hat is askew on its head,
It's taken a tumble—well, that's what I said!
With petals flying in whimsical race,
It giggles, 'Just call it a floral embrace!'

The lettuce stretches, cracks a bold smile,
Saying, 'I've got the most fashionable style!'
As herbs scoff from their kitchen-bound plots,
They're sure they've got the spice that's hot.

Old roots trade puns under cabbage brims,
While zucchini hums some rambunctious hymns.
Together they weave a ridiculous tale,
Of tomatoes and chives, a veggie-scale fail.

Just beneath these leaves, mysteries grow,
Where laughter and colors put on a show.
As life unfolds in its splendid ballet,
The garden's secrets dance, come what may!

Unfolding Mysteries

In the garden, weeds wear hats,
Pretending they're cool, just like the cats.
Gnomes whisper jokes, as daisies sway,
Plotting mischief, come out and play!

A worm jokes about soil's weight,
While ants debate their lunch fate.
Butterflies giggle in the sun's gleam,
Nature's jesters—living the dream.

Tangles of Truth

Vines twist like unkempt hair,
Leaves chuckle, swaying in the air.
A droplet dances on a petal's edge,
Waiting to leap, with a daring pledge.

The sun blinks at the shy old tree,
"Are you hiding a squirrel or is it just me?"
Roots gossip deep in the earth's embrace,
Sharing the tales of the wild, wide space.

Buried Treasures

In soil, a sock and a lost toy car,
Ghosts of childhood, how bizarre!
Raccoons debate, "What's in there?"
Uncovering secrets with a mischievous flair.

A pebble shines, it thinks it's gold,
Tales of adventurers proudly told.
With every dig, laughter explodes,
With nature's whimsy, the fun just unloads.

Silent Germinations

Underneath the ground, secrets hatch,
Mushrooms giggle, a fungal batch.
The seedlings whisper, "We're growing tall!"
While the weeds tease, "You're not tall at all!"

At night, shadows take to the dance,
Mice twirl in the moonlight's trance.
Roots hold meetings, the fungi cheer,
In this quiet, silly frontier!

The Rooted Revelation

In the garden, whispers swirl,
A carrot sings, a turnip twirls.
The lettuce teases, 'Look at me!'
While beets just blush, oh can't you see?

The radish giggles with a grin,
Says, 'My root is where I begin!'
With every sprout, a tale unfolds,
Of garden spies and secrets bold.

The flowers chatter, all aglow,
'Did you hear what the peas know?'
Under leaves, the stories creep,
Like sneaky rabbits, oh so deep.

But as they share, the air gets dense,
A flower shouts, "It makes no sense!"
Yet in this plot, the fun won't fade,
For every secret, a new charade.

Blossoming Secrets

In the meadow, giggles rise,
With daisies playing hide and spies.
A sunflower sways, tall and proud,
While violets whisper, under shroud.

'Come closer, dear,' the tulips call,
'We know the tale, we've seen it all!'
With petals soft, they share a tease,
Of buttercups, and how to please.

The daisies dance in morning light,
Swinging secrets, what a sight!
Behind the grass, the secrets plot,
A bouncing bug, with tales to jot.

But as they laugh, a breeze comes near,
'Oh dear,' says one, 'time to disappear!'
And with a twirl, they vanish quick,
Leaving behind their funny trick.

The Kernel's Tale

In a field, kernels plot and scheme,
Popcorn dreams, they chase and beam.
'What's that noise?' a cob inquires,
'Is it our fate to end in fires?'

The kernels giggle, bounce with glee,
'We're more than snacks, just wait and see!'
With every pop, they burst with flair,
Telling jokes, floating through the air.

'Have you heard the corn's new game?'
'It's hide-and-seek, but who's to blame?'
With husks as cloaks, they hide away,
Just waiting for the perfect day.

But one wise ear, in silence waits,
'The popcorn knows the best of fates!'
In laughter's glow, they churn and roll,
Saying, 'Join us, play a kernel role!'

The Hidden Canopy

Beneath the trees, a world unfolds,
Where whispers blur with tales retold.
A squirrel winks, keeps secrets tight,
While branches sway in sheer delight.

The birds are gossiping at the top,
'Did you see? A leaf just dropped!'
With every rustle, hidden fun,
'Oh look, there goes the morning sun!'

A wise old branch, with knots galore,
Clucks, 'What's this ruckus? Tell me more!'
Beneath, the roots exchange some cheer,
'We've thrilling news, so lend an ear!'

As shadows dance, and sunlight beams,
Their laughter intertwines with dreams.
For in this canopy, bright and free,
The joy of secrets, is glee's decree.

Furtive Twists

In the garden, where gnomes hide,
A carrot dreams of a leafy ride.
Tomatoes gossip, oh what a sight,
Splashing colors in morning light.

Behind a fence, the radishes sneak,
Planning a party, so unique.
Peas in pods chuckle, what a crew,
Inventing dances in shades of dew.

The spinach sings of a swirling dance,
While dancing beetroot takes the chance.
Cabbage whispers all kinds of lore,
As the pumpkins roll, asking for more.

Secret meetings in the soft, dark soil,
Where worms plot ways to make it all royal.
Nature's jesters, with smiles so wide,
In the funny garden where secrets reside.

The Enchanted Bud

In a pot where daffodils sway,
A tiny bud hatches plans for play.
It swears to bloom by next Sunday,
But keeps on napping, in a funny way.

Around it, daisies giggle and cheer,
While lazy herbs lounge, sipping beer.
The tulips tease, calling them slow,
As the sunlight dances, putting on a show.

But when the moon peeks out with a grin,
All the blooms gather, let the fun begin!
They twirl and spin in the cool night air,
Sprouting laughter, without a care.

From hidden corners, the laughter spreads,
As flowers weave tales of garden beds.
In bloom's delightful, quirky woods,
The enchanted bud giggles with sprightly moods.

Whispers of Renewal

In the meadow where dandelions chuckle,
Whispers of laughter mix with a shuffle.
The ants parade in their tiny shoes,
Sharing the gossip, the grass sings the blues.

A squirrel breaks into a nimble twirl,
While mushrooms giggle in a topsy swirl.
The breeze tells tales of the blooms' big dreams,
As the petals shimmer in sunlight beams.

When bees buzz in their raucous flight,
It's a dance-off in the warm sunlight.
The daisies are judges, with a board and pen,
Ranking the best moves again and again.

Nature connives with a wink and a grin,
In this secret world where tomfoolery begins.
Renewal is funny, will have you in stitches,
As every sprout flaunts its little quirks and glitches.

Growing in Silence

In a corner where no one peeks,
Plants have parties, sharing their tweaks.
With silent giggles and mischievous glee,
They swap their soil recipes, oh how silly!

The thistles boast of their prickly charms,
While clovers share secrets, full of farms.
Whispers float in the softly cooled air,
As sunflowers giggle, without a care.

A wilted leaf tells of adventures grand,
Of dancing with wind in a far-off land.
And in the shadows, the herbs throw a bash,
With minty drinks in a jazzy splash.

So, if you stroll by, lend an ear,
To the quiet laughter that's always near.
For growing in silence, it seems so wise,
Hides a world bursting with fun in disguise.

www.ingramcontent.com/pod-product-compliance
Lightning Source LLC
Chambersburg PA
CBHW051632160426
43209CB00004B/621